SCIENCE IN OUR WORLD

WEATHER

Contributory Author
Brian Knapp, BSc, PhD
Art Director
Duncan McCrae, BSc
Special photography
Graham Servante
Special models
*Tim Fulford, MA, Head of Design and Technology,
Leighton Park School*
Editorial consultants
Anna Grayson, Rita Owen
Science advisor
*Jack Brettle, BSc, PhD, Chief Research Scientist,
Pilkington plc*
Illustrators
David Hardy, Mark Franklin
Production controller
Gillian Gatehouse
Print consultants
Landmark Production Consultants Ltd
Printed and bound in Hong Kong
Produced by *EARTHSCAPE EDITIONS*

First published in the United Kingdom in 1991
by Atlantic Europe Publishing Company Limited
86 Peppard Road, Sonning Common, Reading,
Berkshire, RG4 9RP, UK
Tel: (0734) 723751   Fax: (0734) 724488

British Library Cataloguing in Publication Data
Knapp, Brian
    Weather
    1. Weather – For Children
    I. Title   II. Series
    551.5

        ISBN 1-869860-35-7

In this book you will find some words that have been shown in **bold** type. There is a full explanation of each of these words on pages 46 and 47.

On many pages you will find experiments that you might like to try for yourself. They have been put in a coloured box like this.

Acknowledgements
The publishers would like to thank the following:
Martin Morris, Stephen Pitcher, Leighton Park
School, Redlands County Primary School,
Berkshire County Council School Library
Service and Oxfordshire County Council
Education Department.

Picture credits
t=top b= bottom l=left r=right

All photographs from the Earthscape Editions
photographic library except the following:
Allsport 5, 21; Keith Wheeler 4, 31b; NASA 5, 9,
34-35; Science Photo Library 4, 25, 28, 32b;
University of Dundee 43b; ZEFA 33t, 33b.

0385

*   3   8   5   *

**This book is to be returned on or before
the last date stamped below.**

Contents

Introduction

rain
page 26

cloud types
page 22

fog
page 18

snow
page 32

clouds from space
page 24

frost
page 30

Look out of the window. Is it cloudy or sunny? Does it feel warm or cold? Does the air feel moist or dry? Is it raining? Is it calm or windy?

All these changes in the air, which is called the **atmosphere**, are important. Together they go to make up the **weather**.

The weather is a general word to mean how warm or cold it is; how wet or dry it is, whether the Sun is shining or if its cloudy, if it is windy and how moist the air feels.

Wherever you live the weather affects your life. It affects the things you do, the clothes you wear, the house you live in and even how you get about. Fine weather helps to make your holidays fun and sometimes bad weather spoils your games.

Sun
page 6

forecasting
page 42

cities
page 38

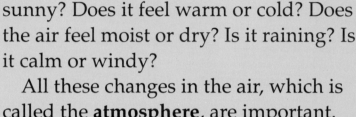

thermometers
page 10

world weather
page 8

storm
page 34

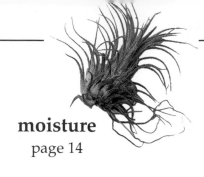

moisture
page 14

hot air
page 20

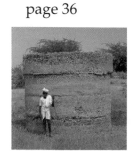

dew
page 16

In this book you will discover many interesting and exciting things about our weather. You will find out what makes the weather and how this affects our lives. You will discover why some weather is good and why it occasionally spells disaster. And you will discover how important the weather is to people, plants and animals.

You will also discover that people can have an important influence on the weather – sometimes it is for good, sometimes bad.

On this page you can see some of the ways the weather affects people all over the world. To make your discoveries just turn to the page of your choice.

drought
page 36

greenhouse weather
page 44

mountains
page 40

wind
page 12

lightning
page 28

When the Sun shines

Without the heat from the Sun, the Earth would be cold and frozen. How much sunshine we receive and how warm it is also depends on where we are on Earth. The closer we are to the **equator**, the hotter it is and the closer to the North or South **Pole**, the colder it is. The amount of heat we receive from the Sun also changes with the seasons and through the day.

The Sun at noon
If you live near the equator the Sun will be directly overhead at noon and it will be hot. But the farther you live from the equator, the lower the noon-day Sun will be in the sky and the cooler it will be.

The polar regions have ice and snow all year because the noon-day Sun is always low in the sky.

Beach ball Earth

You can see the difference the height of the Sun makes by using a torch (to show the Sun's rays) and a beach ball or similar large ball (to show the Earth).

In a darkened room hold a torch about arm's length from the beach ball. Now shine the torch on the middle of the ball and draw round the place lit by the beam. It will be a circle like the one shown here.

Next hold the torch a little higher so that the beam shines near the top of the ball. The beam will spread out in an oval shape. Draw this shape too. Which is the bigger shape?

The same amount of light fell on each place, so where it spread over a bigger area it will have less heating power.

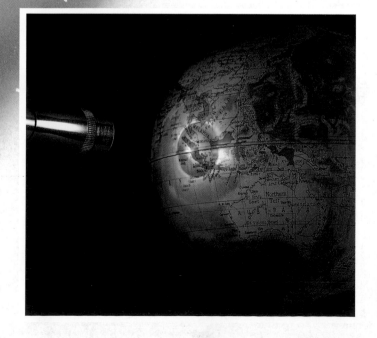

World weather

Had you ever wondered why the weather was different in one part of the world from another? Do you know why some people have long hot dry summers while other people get rain all year round?

Many of these differences are because of the way the Sun's heat causes the air and clouds to swirl round the world.

Weather attraction
The Sun brings people to the **tropics**. This is the place where the air becomes hot and starts to rise. Although these holiday-makers cannot see it, hot, moist air is rising all around them. From here it spreads outwards to the rest of the world.

Swirling warmth
Air swirls in the atmosphere just like water swirls in a bowl. To see the effect, take a clear bowl of water and stir it up with a spoon. Now drop a small amount of dye crystals in the water in one place. Slowly the colour trail will wind round and round, showing how the swirling water mixes.

The atmosphere is swirled by the spinning of the Earth. As a result, hot air from the tropics can be carried all the way to the Poles.

Caused by the Sun

World weather patterns are caused by the Sun. The Sun does not just make one place hotter than another. It also has a big effect on the pattern of the world's clouds, and where and when it rains.

Hot air spreads out and sinks over the deserts and no clouds form

Sahara Desert

Africa

Hot air rises to produce these blotchy clouds. Each one is a thunderstorm

Huge swirls of cloud form in the cooler regions of the world. These clouds give long periods of rain

Connections

All parts of the world are connected together by the swirling air. The pattern of **clouds** (which show white on this picture) give you some clues to how the air swirls about. However, much air moves unseen.

The air is cold and clear over the South Pole

Antarctica

9

The warmth of the air

We describe the warmth of the air by its temperature. We measure temperature with a **thermometer**.

Most people feel comfortable if the temperature is about 20-25 °Celsius (write a C for short). This is the temperature of many living-rooms and offices.

It is difficult to sit comfortably if the temperature is below 15 °C even if you are well wrapped up.

Scale in degrees Celsius

Red liquid (alcohol)

Liquid thermometer
Liquids become bigger, or expand, as they get warm and shrink, or contract, when they get colder.

In a thermometer the liquid is trapped in a very small tube and this makes any changes easier to see.

Most of the liquid is in the bulb at the bottom. As the air warms, it heats the liquid. The only way the liquid can expand is by rising up the tube. So the height of the liquid in the tube tells us how warm the air is.

Bulb

Find out how warm it is
You will need a simple liquid thermometer, like the one shown on the top of the page opposite.

Place your thermometer in a safe, shady, dry place. Ask a grown-up to fix it safely in a spot where it is easy to read. Keep a record of the temperatures on a chart for each day.

Each day try guessing the temperature and then read the thermometer. Get your friends to guess as well.

See if you can find the lowest temperature at which you can sit comfortably. It varies a little between people.

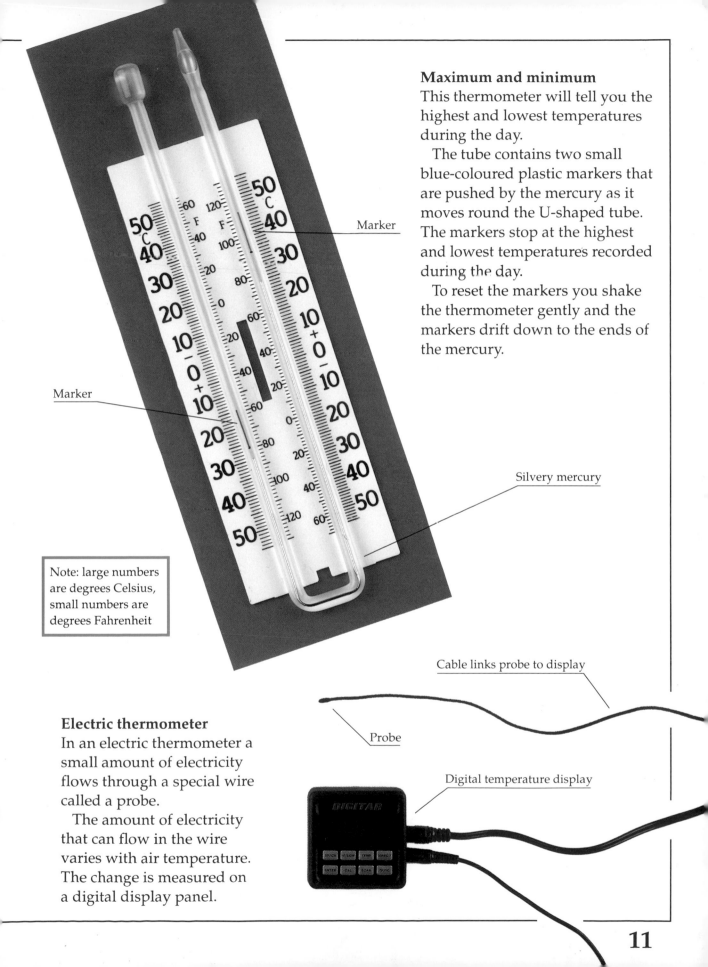

Maximum and minimum
This thermometer will tell you the highest and lowest temperatures during the day.

The tube contains two small blue-coloured plastic markers that are pushed by the mercury as it moves round the U-shaped tube. The markers stop at the highest and lowest temperatures recorded during the day.

To reset the markers you shake the thermometer gently and the markers drift down to the ends of the mercury.

Marker

Marker

Silvery mercury

Note: large numbers are degrees Celsius, small numbers are degrees Fahrenheit

Cable links probe to display

Probe

Digital temperature display

Electric thermometer
In an electric thermometer a small amount of electricity flows through a special wire called a probe.

The amount of electricity that can flow in the wire varies with air temperature. The change is measured on a digital display panel.

11

When the winds blow

Air is very rarely still. Gentle movements of the air are called **breezes**. A cool breeze on a hot sunny day is very pleasant. Stronger movements are called **winds**.

The wind scale
You can see which way the wind is blowing by looking at a weather-vane on top of a building.

You can find out how much wind there is by using a small device with cups that catch the wind. It is called an anemometer. An automatic wind station is shown here.

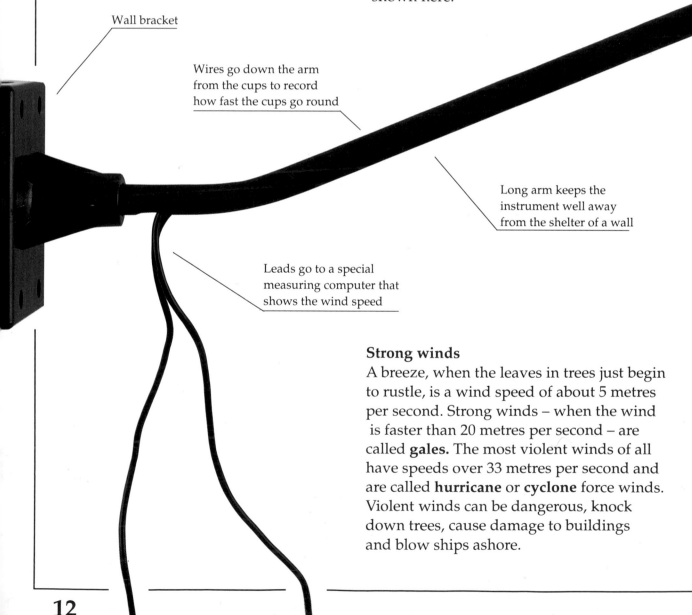

Wall bracket

Wires go down the arm from the cups to record how fast the cups go round

Long arm keeps the instrument well away from the shelter of a wall

Leads go to a special measuring computer that shows the wind speed

Strong winds
A breeze, when the leaves in trees just begin to rustle, is a wind speed of about 5 metres per second. Strong winds – when the wind is faster than 20 metres per second – are called **gales.** The most violent winds of all have speeds over 33 metres per second and are called **hurricane** or **cyclone** force winds. Violent winds can be dangerous, knock down trees, cause damage to buildings and blow ships ashore.

Vane turns on a spindle to show the wind direction. The large part of the blade faces down wind and the small part points into the wind

Cups that catch the wind

Measure the wind

The wind can easily be measured using a wind sock. You will find large wind socks at airports.

To make a wind sock like the one shown on the left, you need a tube of lightweight material such as nylon, a piece of wire and a stick.

Make a circle of wire to keep the end of the sock open and stitch the sock to the wire. Tie the sock to a pole using a loop of string as in the picture.

When the wind blows the wind sock will fill with air and rise clear of the pole; the stronger the wind, the higher the end will rise. The foot end of the sock will point away from the wind.

Moisture in the air

Water is all around us. It is in the air we breathe as well as the sky outside. Most of the time you cannot see it because it is in the form of an invisible gas called **water vapour**. Water vapour is sometimes known as **moisture**.

Sensing moisture

If there is a lot of moisture in the air it feels very humid. If there is little moisture the air feels dry and we soon become thirsty. Moisture in the air is also the source of rain.

Sources of moisture

Most of the water vapour in the air evaporates from the seas and rivers, and from plants growing on the land.

Trapping evaporation

To trap the water from plants put a clear plastic bag around some leaves on a tree branch.

Choose a sunny day and then watch the water appear. Within a few minutes the inside of the plastic will be steaming up. If you hadn't trapped it, all that water would have become moisture in the air.

Air strainers

In some parts of the world the forests are always full of moisture. In these places some plants do not have any roots. Instead they soak up all the moisture they need through their leaves. These are commonly called 'air plants'.

Air plants are popular house plants. Perhaps you already have one at home.

Disappearing water

A saucer of water will turn to water vapour and disappear as if by magic. This is called **evaporation**.

Look for evaporated in the kitchen. Steam is concentrated water vapour cooling down and forming droplets.

There is little steam in the rest of the room because it is has been soaked up by the air and remains invisible water vapour.

Towers of steam

Power stations use water to cool the generators. The steamy air in the towers makes clouds when it leaves the top.

The huge white plume that stretches up to the clouds is man-made – it is the cloud produced as the water, which has turned to steam, leaves the power station's cooling towers.

15

Drops of dew

When warm moist air brushes against a cold window or a glass of cold liquid, some of the air cools and turns into tiny droplets of water. This is called **condensation**.

Sometimes the droplets get bigger and run down the glass to make pools of water. This shows you there is a lot of water vapour in the air.

What dew tells us

The amount of dew depends on the overnight weather. When the air cools rapidly during the night the dew will probably be heavy.

Dew can only form if there is a lot of moisture in the air. So dew tells us that the overnight air was moist as well as cold.

How dew forms

Condensation outdoors is called **dew**. Dew is the carpet of small droplets of water that cover grass and other cold surfaces near the ground.

Dew forms whenever something gets cold during the night. Then, as the air brushes against it some water vapour changes into droplets of water.

In this early morning picture you can see how the tips of the leaves have collected drops of water overnight.

Collect condensation

This picture shows you how you could collect dew using a polythene sheet. The sheet is pegged up on four sticks and a stone placed in the centre to make a cone.

Place a cup *under* the centre of the sheet and leave it overnight. Does water collect on top of the sheet or in the cup? Can you think why?

In desert countries dew may be the only source of moisture. In some countries long lines of plastic sheets collect dew and small holes in the sheets allow the water to drip down to water the crops.

Why dew disappears

Dew rarely lasts for long in summer because the warmth of the Sun turns the dew back into water vapour. You can sometimes see surfaces steaming as the moisture evaporates from them.

Polythene sheet

Stone

Collecting cup

In the fog

Fog is simply a cloud on the ground. All clouds are made of millions of tiny water droplets. Each droplet absorbs sound, so if you walk about in foggy weather everything seems unusually quiet.

If you walk through a fog you brush against the droplets and it quickly makes your hair, face and clothes wet.

Sea fog
Sea fog forms over a cold sea and then gets blown inland. It can form even in the day.

This picture of San Francisco's Golden Gate Bridge on the Pacific coast of the USA shows sea fog creeping from right to left during an afternoon in autumn. A few minutes after this picture was taken the whole bridge was covered in fog.

Why land fog occurs

Fog only happens when very moist air near the ground cools down. The moist air condenses and forms into millions of tiny water droplets.

Land fog usually starts on the ground, but as more of the air cools down the fog thickens in an upwards direction. On a foggy night you may first see it swirling round your feet, before it thickens and covers everything in sight. By morning it may only leave the tops of trees or hills in clear air.

How far can you see?

The reason you cannot see very far in a fog is because many millions of water droplets are in the way. The more water droplets there are, the shorter the distance you can see.

The densest fog has so many water droplets that you can hardly see your hand in front of your face. The thinnest fog is called **mist**. In this case there are fewer water droplets.

Fog can be dangerous when it forms in patches such as near a river or in a valley bottom. Drivers can be in clear air one moment and then drive straight into a bank of fog where they can hardly see at all. Driving quickly in the fog soon leads to accidents.

How clouds are made

Fully grown clouds

Clouds are made of millions of tiny water droplets which have been made high in the sky.

Clouds begin to form when moist warm air rises from near the ground. Rising air is invisible, but we can easily prove that hot air rises, and even follow the way air rises by looking at hot-air balloons.

Clouds in the sky

Warm air often rises unseen from the ground. The first time the warm air can be seen is when moisture forms in the cooling air and it becomes a cloud.

Clouds grow from tiny patches. It then takes between a few minutes and an hour for a cloud to grow to its full size.

A full sized cloud usually only lives for an hour or two. At the end of this time there is no heat left in the air and the cloud fades away and is replaced by new clouds.

Look towards the <u>top</u> of *one* cloud on a sunny day when there are just a few 'pillow-shaped' clouds in the sky. Over a few minutes you will see the 'pillows' grow and change shape as the hot air pushes up and up.

Pillows growing strongly

The first signs of clouds

Copying clouds

Hot-air balloons are the big colourful balloons that drift through the sky. The way they move helps us to understand the way clouds behave.

Hot air is lighter than cold air and a the hot air in balloon will therefore lift it off the ground.

Hot air balloons drift in the sky, carried along by natural breezes. They can stay up only as long as the balloon contains warm air.

Gas being burned

Balloon fills with hot air

Basket

Cloud watch

Clouds can tell us much about what is going on in the air. If you become good at cloud watching you can even tell what weather lies ahead.

Pillow clouds that tell of a fine sunny day
Fluffy white **cumulus** clouds are common in a summer sky.

Watch them carefully during the morning. If they do not grow then the day will be fine. If they gradually grow and cover the sky, showers may occur in the afternoon. If they grow very quickly then you can be sure there are storms ahead.

Thick flat clouds that spell rain
This overcast sky is made of thick dark grey clouds. There are no fair weather 'pillows' to be seen.

This kind of cloud is called **stratus**. When you see it you know you are in for wet, and even stormy weather that may last for many hours.

Thunderclouds

Just before a storm you may see clouds that seem to grow higher than you can see. These are 'skyscrapers' of the air, reaching upwards for many thousands of metres. Thunder, lightning and hailstones are the features of these tall storm clouds called **cumulonimbus**.

Inside a storm cloud the air is moving upwards very fast and only the largest drops of rain can fall out. This is the reason that thunderstorms are often accompanied by large raindrops that splash when they reach the ground. The long grey streaks that stretch from the bottom of a thundercloud are made by torrential rain.

Trails and wispy clouds in a clear sky

Wispy clouds high in the sky are called **cirrus** clouds. They spell fine, settled weather. They are made of scattered ice crystals that are being moved around by gentle breezes.

Sometimes high-flying aeroplanes make straight white trails in the sky when the moisture from their engines cools into ice. These are man-made cirrus clouds.

Clouds seen from space

We are used to seeing clouds from below. From space we can look at the tops of the clouds and the patterns that they make across the sky.

The blue planet

From space the Earth is a blue planet. There are blue oceans broken up by the brown of land, all criss-crossed with streaks of white cloud.

Look carefully and you will see many different patterns. Across Africa there are lots of white blobs. Each of these is a mighty thunderstorm.

Near the top and bottom of the picture you can see great swirling shaped clouds that are bringing bad weather.

In between the two great areas of cloud there is clear sky. Here are the deserts.

Now look to see what the weather is like around the world.

North America
Great banks of layer cloud cover the eastern coast, giving widespread rain

Showers over the ocean
Wherever you see a pattern of many small clouds, you know that the weather is showery. Each white patch is a thunder cloud, but the blue piece in between is clear sunny sky

Amazonia in Brazil
This cloudy area lies over the Amazonian rainforest. The huge area of forest releases so much moisture into the air that it creates its own clouds and rain

South American Andes
The high Andes mountains run down the west coast of this continent and keep much of the cloud out in the western sea

Antarctica
Antarctica is covered with ice thousands of metres thick. Here the weather is always cold and only snow falls. Fierce winds develop and blizzards are common

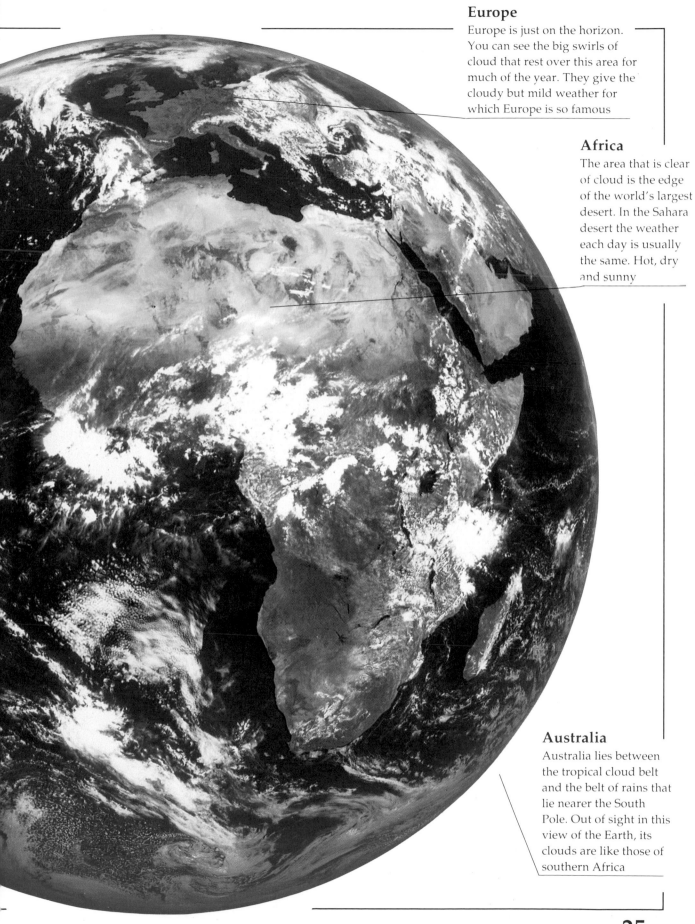

Europe

Europe is just on the horizon. You can see the big swirls of cloud that rest over this area for much of the year. They give the cloudy but mild weather for which Europe is so famous

Africa

The area that is clear of cloud is the edge of the world's largest desert. In the Sahara desert the weather each day is usually the same. Hot, dry and sunny

Australia

Australia lies between the tropical cloud belt and the belt of rains that lie nearer the South Pole. Out of sight in this view of the Earth, its clouds are like those of southern Africa

Rain and hail

Everyone knows that dark, grey clouds means wet weather. But the water that comes from a cloud may be of many kinds. Here is what you can expect to find.

Types of water

Raindrops form when many tiny water droplets in a cloud come together and fall. Sometimes raindrops will be large and fall with such force that they splash up from the ground; on other occasions there will be only a form of light rain known as **drizzle**.

Rain and drizzle are two types of **precipitation** – forms of water that fall from clouds. The other forms of precipitation are **snow**, a partly melted kind of snow called **sleet** and **hail**.

Every form of precipitation falls from the same types of clouds; the differences are mainly caused by the thickness and coldness of the cloud.

Torrents

The hotter the air, the more moisture it can hold and the larger the amount of rain that falls. Rainfall in the tropics can be torrential and fall so hard that it bounces up over a metre from the ground. Here you see it cascading off a roof during a wet season storm in the tropics.

Rain

People often draw raindrops in the shape of teardrops, like water dripping from a tap. But real raindrops fall quickly through the air and this makes them more doughnut-shaped.

It is difficult to see rain drops because they fall so quickly. You can get an idea of how big the raindrops are by trying to copy the splash that they make. Try dripping water by shaking drops from the end of a pencil that you have dipped in water.

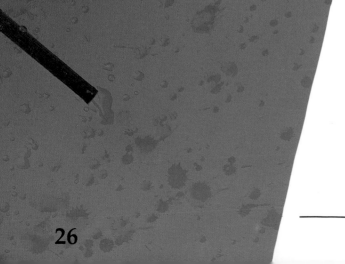

Use a bottle like this

Measuring rain

Scientists collect rain very carefully in special containers. They are called rain gauges. But you can get a good idea of the rain that falls by making your own rain gauge.

Ask a grown-up to cut a soft drink bottle in half. You can use the top as a funnel by turning it upside down like the one shown here. The steep sides of the funnel stop water splashing in or out.

To stop the raingauge blowing over in the wind, dig a hole deep enough to bury a flower pot up to its rim, then stand the raingauge inside it.

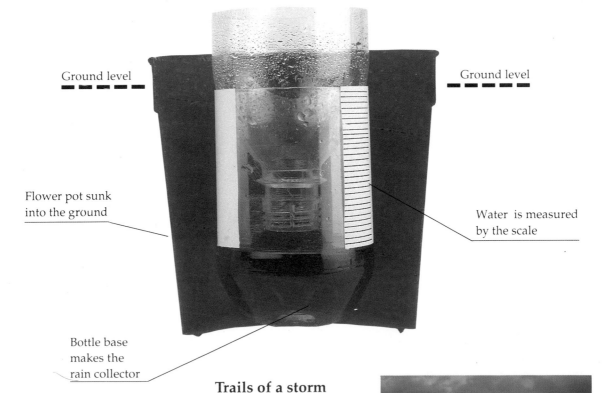

Upturned top makes the funnel

Ground level

Ground level

Flower pot sunk into the ground

Water is measured by the scale

Bottle base makes the rain collector

Trails of a storm

This storm is releasing so much rain that you can see it falling from the bottom of the thickest part of the cloud.

Thunder and lightning

Storms can be really scary. You see a flash of light and then a hair-raising boom of thunder follows a few seconds later.

If you can't ignore the storm there's something you can do. You can work out how far away the storm is and if it is coming in your direction.

Lightning flash
The lightning flash from a cloud may last for nearly a second. This is why we sometimes see lightning so clearly.

In the picture below, a camera has captured several lightning flashes over a town in Australia.

How lightning strikes

A bolt of **lightning** is an enormous electrical spark. Sometimes the flash is a single giant spark, but most often it is made up of three or four rapid sparks.

The path of the flash is very jagged as you can see in this photograph. These short darting lines show how the lightning is finding a path through the air.

Thunderclap

The lightning spark heats the air and sends out great shock waves. When the shock waves reach us we hear it as the sound called **thunder**.

Sometimes the thunder is a single deafening clap. This happens when the lightning is close to us. At other times we hear a long roll or rumble. This happens when the shock wave is bounced between the bottom of the clouds and the ground, giving echoes.

Dark clouds

Thunder and lightning can only come from the tallest clouds. Often you can tell a thunderstorm is about to break because the sky goes dark grey, as in this picture.

Find out how far thunder is from you

Count in seconds from when you see the lightning flash (count 'one thousand and one, one thousand and two . . . etc. or use a stop watch).

Stop when you hear the thunder. Divide the time counted by three to get the distance in kilometres between you and the lightning.

Do the calculation every time you see a lightning flash. Longer counts mean the storm is moving away, shorter counts mean the storm is getting nearer.

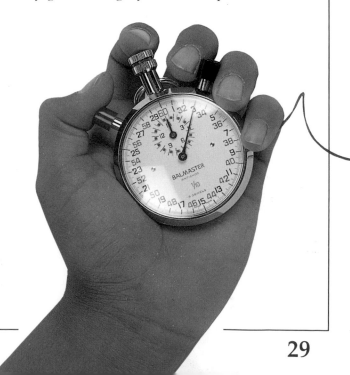

Sparkling frost

In many parts of the world, winter brings some frosty days. They happen when there are clear cloud-free nights and the ground can lose heat quickly.

The air nearest the cold ground soon cools and forms dew. The drops of dew then freeze into **frost**. On the coldest nights the moisture in the air turns directly into ice. At these times the ice builds into long delicate crystals.

Where frost bites hardest

This picture shows a wire fence that has been made quite solid by frost.

This kind of frost is called rime. It only grows when the air is bitterly cold and very moist – the sort of thing you get in high mountains or in the polar regions.

Frosty weather in the freezer

Fridges and freezers are good places to look for frost when it is not cold outside. Fridges and freezers are kept cold to preserve food. But every time the door is opened some cold air flows out and warm, moist kitchen air flows in. As the warm air touches the cold sides of the freezing compartment the water vapour begins to form frost.

See how much frost you can find in your fridge or freezer. Sometimes freezers get so much frost the lid will not shut. Ask a grown-up to show you the frost in your freezer. Look closely and try to spot the ice crystals on the sides near the top.

Growing frost

Frost is made of tiny ice crystals just like snowflakes. Look closely and you can see them standing up from the leaf in this picture.

Also look for frost making exciting patterns on window panes.

Pockets of cold

Just as cold air pours out when you open the door of a fridge, so frosty air formed during the night rolls down slopes and settles in hollows.

Hollows where the frosty air comes to rest and builds up are called frost pockets. The most common places are valley bottoms and near to ponds and steams. In these places the air feels colder in the evening and the white frosty glaze lasts well into the morning.

Snowy weather

Snow is made high in the coldest parts of clouds, then it gently flutters to the ground as delicate crystals of ice.

Snow can build up on the trees and even break branches with its weight. On the roads it can bring danger and in towns it can be a great nuisance. But snowy weather can also bring a lot of fun.

Snowflakes

A **snowflake** begins to grow as a tiny ice crystal around a small speck of dust in the cloud. An ice crystal grows in a regular repeating pattern. You can see some of the patterns in this picture. Ice crystals are as light as feathers and they are easily kept up in the air by swirling winds. In a thick cloud ice crystals mix together and stick to one another. When they are big enough the collection of crystals – a snowflake – falls gently to the ground as snow.

When snow falls

Snow settles into thick carpets when the wind is light. But winter storms can also bring strong winds. Each falling snowflake is like a sail in this wind. It has very little weight but it is broad and flat. The wind catches the flakes and drives them forward. This makes a **blizzard**.

When the wind meets an obstacle such as a wall or fence, it is swirled round and round. Snow builds up behind obstacles to form deep snow drifts.

Snow drifts can be many metres high and they can bury cars completely.

Sporting snow

Snow can be good fun. Each year many people go to places that have snowy winters. The best weather for winter sports is a mixture of sunny days – when people can enjoy the skiing – and scattered heavy snowstorms to replace the snow that has been worn away.

Storm!

Sometimes the weather can be very violent and cause much destruction and loss of life.

In places where storm-force winds are common, people learn to live with the danger and take many special measures to protect themselves.

What cyclones can do
The spiralling clouds shown in the picture above belong to a cyclone. On the ground the winds can reach over 100 kilometres an hour. They can drive the sea on to the land causing widespread flooding, uproot trees and destroy buildings and crops.

Tropical storms

Cyclones – severe tropical storms – are also called **hurricanes** in America and **typhoons** in the west Pacific.

They start as simple thunderstorms over warm oceans but quickly grow to be huge spiralling masses of cloud hundreds of kilometres across.

There is a season for cyclones. In the USA it is between September and November; in the west Pacific it is between December and May. At these times, the weather service keeps a cyclone watch to give warning of storms that may be approaching.

Why cyclones die

Cyclones are fuelled by the heat from warm seas. As they drift onto land they lose this source of power and slowly get weaker until they eventually fade away. Unfortunately this only happens after several days of havoc and destruction.

Storms that catch the unwary

In places where severe storms are rare, people are not so prepared and their homes are not built to protect them.

When severe storms hit these areas they can therefore cause enormous damage. Large ships are driven on to beaches, roofs are torn from houses and trees are blown down across roads.

Drought

A long dry spell of weather is usually welcomed. It brings fine, sunny and settled weather when the temperature is high and people can spend all their time outdoors.

But if the dry weather lasts for too long then a **drought** sets in and many people, plants and animals may suffer.

Animal hardship

In places where there are large areas of open grassland, a long drought can quickly bring disaster and many animals may die. In the wild, animals move away – or migrate – from areas of drought, often by walking vast distances. That is what the buffalo shown in the picture below would have done in the past.

Today, as with domesticated animals, the buffalo are fenced in and they depend on man-made waterholes and wind-driven water pumps to provide their water and food.

Coping with dry weather

People get used to the amount of rain they can rely on. They make sure the way they live matches their water supply.

To cope with a long dry spell farmers plant special types of crops that grow and ripen quickly. This barley has short stems so that it can reach its full height without taking a lot of moisture from the soil.

Drought and the land

During a drought the grass stops growing and no longer protects the soil from winds. In this picture you can see how much soil was stripped away in a drought. The man is standing by a well. He used to be able to reach into it to get water. Since the soil was lost in a drought the well is now completely out of reach.

Patchwork of brown

A landscape of drought shows clearly from the air. The grass, with its short roots, quickly becomes parched and turns brown. The trees, with their deeper roots, can usually find water. As a result their leaves remain green.

City weather

Cities have a surprisingly important effect on the local weather. Trees, grass and open fields are replaced by buildings and roads.

As people want warmer buildings and more cars, city weather gets less and less like the weather of the countryside. In winter, especially, the city is an 'island' of heat within a countryside of cold.

Warmth check

Find out about your home weather. Make a reading – using a thermometer like the one on page 10 – just outside your front door. Now make another reading in your garden or in an open space near your house. Is it warmer or cooler away from the house.

Now find out if the temperature changes as you walk along the street. Use the thermometer again, noting down each reading you make and where you made it. If there are changes can you see what they are caused by? Try the same records at the weekend as well as on a working day, and also on a calm day and a windy one.

Signs of a warm city

It is easy to see how much warmer a city can be by looking at the flowers and trees.

In spring the city warms faster than the country, leaves form and flowers bloom weeks before they emerge in the countryside.

When all the leaves in the countryside have fallen in autumn, many trees in the city streets still keep theirs. This is because the temperature has not fallen enough to make plants think that autumn has arrived.

All in all it gives city dwellers a shorter winter – which is good news.

A mix of good and bad

Cities alter weather considerably,
especially when there are large buildings
close together. Look at the picture below
and you will see some of both the good
and bad weather changes. Perhaps you
can think of some more.

People in the highest
parts of the buildings
may find themselves
in the clouds or fog

Heat from air
conditioning and
heating plants is
pumped into the air

Tall buildings
trap the heat and
keep days and
nights warm

Tall buildings in
straight lines funnel
the wind. Strong
gusts can make
walking difficult at
street corners

Cars send out heat
and pollution at
ground level.
Pollution gives
sore throats and
runny eyes

Hills in cities cause
cold air to drain
down the slopes

Without plants,
city air is very dry

Mountain weather

Mountains can make their own weather. As air blows over them it can be funnelled through valleys and whisked over the peaks. Rising air cools and can easily produce cloud and rain.

Altogether mountain weather is less settled, more cloudy, colder and wetter than the surrounding countryside.

Wet side, dry side
The two sides of a mountain range can have completely different types of weather. On the side which faces the winds it can be cloudy and wet while on the side away from the wind it may be sunny and dry. This is because the mountains block the rain-bearing winds. The dry side of a range is called the rain shadow.

This picture shows clouds forming on the mountains while it is sunny and dry in the valley below.

Nowhere to hide
Mountains are often very exposed places with steep, barren slopes that do not provide shelter for animals or plants.

These people are crossing a pass in the Himalaya mountains of Asia at about 6000 metres above sea level. Snow still lies in patches near their route. Even in the height of summer nights spent camping near snow can be bitterly cold.

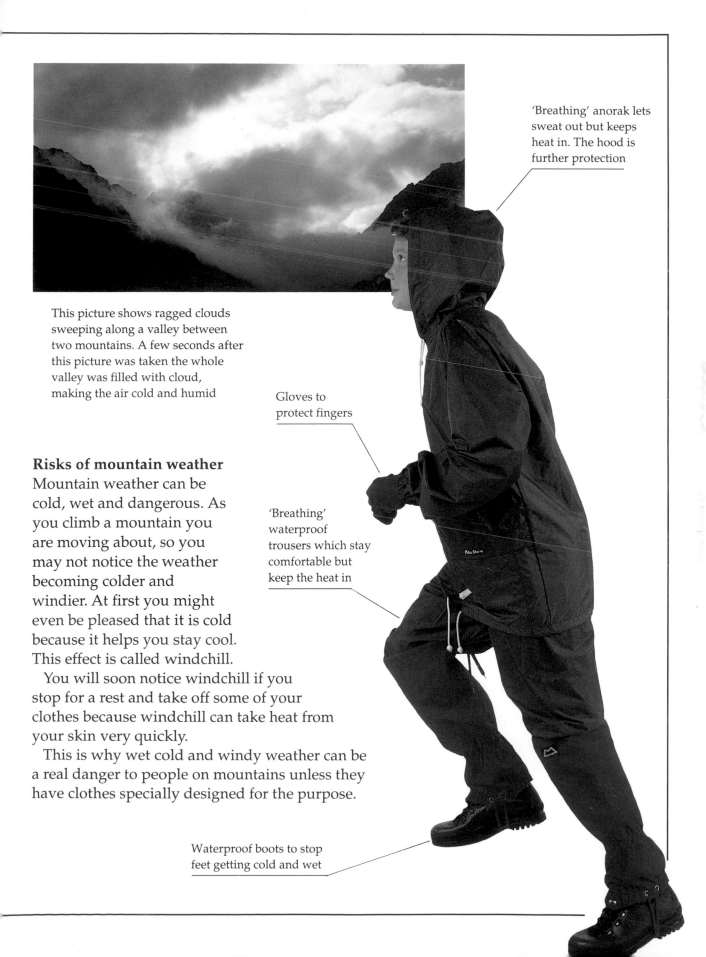

'Breathing' anorak lets sweat out but keeps heat in. The hood is further protection

This picture shows ragged clouds sweeping along a valley between two mountains. A few seconds after this picture was taken the whole valley was filled with cloud, making the air cold and humid

Gloves to protect fingers

'Breathing' waterproof trousers which stay comfortable but keep the heat in

Risks of mountain weather

Mountain weather can be cold, wet and dangerous. As you climb a mountain you are moving about, so you may not notice the weather becoming colder and windier. At first you might even be pleased that it is cold because it helps you stay cool. This effect is called windchill.

You will soon notice windchill if you stop for a rest and take off some of your clothes because windchill can take heat from your skin very quickly.

This is why wet cold and windy weather can be a real danger to people on mountains unless they have clothes specially designed for the purpose.

Waterproof boots to stop feet getting cold and wet

Forecasting the weather

Weather forecasting is important for many people. Here are some typical questions we ask about the weather: 'Will it turn cold and icy on the roads? Shall we take a raincoat with us today? Is the sports match likely to be cancelled because of snow? Is there a cyclone on the horizon? Will the dry spell end?' A lot of effort goes into trying to give the answers.

Nature's signs

Some people can use natural changes to tell the weather. If you stand a fir cone on an outside windowledge it will open as the weather turns dry and close as wet conditions approach.

It wont forecast very far ahead, but it's good fun to watch.

Do it yourself

People have tried to tell the future weather for centuries. Many people have made up rhymes to help such as:

'Red sky at night, shepherd's delight; red sky in the morning, shepherd's warning'.' Use the pages in this book to forecast the weather for a few hours ahead. Look at the sky to find the type of cloud and then read off the weather that can be expected from pages 22 and 23.

If the weather turns and it rains unexpectedly you could be in for a soaking. But is it fair to blame the weather forecasters?

Home barometer

You can tell a lot about the way the weather will change by looking at your home or school **barometer**. This is an instrument for telling how the air pressure is changing. If the pressure is going up, the weather will be fine and dry; if the pressure is going down, expect cloud and rain.

Answering the questions

Many countries in the world have a team of people to forecast the weather. They use information from the ground and satellites in space.

Satellites send back detailed pictures which can be used to keep track of clouds and storms. This picture shows the swirling clouds of a tropical storm in the Gulf of Mexico. It will help forecasters to give accurate storm warnings.

Weather forecaster

The weather forecaster's task is to explain the pattern of weather in a simple way. To get as accurate as possible the forecast is made up from thousands of observations and fed into super computers. To make all this information easily understood the forecaster uses charts with symbols.

Weather charts look roughly the same all over the world. Look closely at the weather forecast on your TV channel and find out what symbols your weather forecaster uses.

Greenhouse weather

It may seem incredible to think that each of us can affect the world's weather. But there are now nearly six billion people in the world and together they can make a big difference to the atmosphere and thus to our weather.

Sun's rays

Power at a price
In the past much carbon dioxide was also locked away in the rocks, as **fossil fuels** – coal, oil and gas.

We are now burning the fossil fuels to run our cars and power our homes – and putting millions of tons of carbon dioxide into the air each year as a result.

Less heat gets back to space

Carbon dioxide in the atmosphere helps trap heat from the Earth

Our greenhouse world
All the weather in the world depends on the atmosphere. It is a special mix of gases that let the heat from the Sun come in, but which act like a blanket to slow down any heat going out. The effect is much like the way a greenhouse works.

The atmosphere is easily upset by changing the mix of gases, especially one called carbon dioxide. The more carbon dioxide there is in the air the greater the warming greenhouse effect becomes.

Carbon dioxide holds the key

Carbon dioxide is released when any kind of fuel is burned. Every time you light a tiny match you are releasing carbon dioxide because you are burning part of a tree.

Warmer weather?

What will the weather be like in a 'greenhouse world'? Many places will be warmer, but here are some problems that may lie in store.

Some of the best farmland – such as the American prairies – may become *deserts*. This could lead to a world shortage of food.

If all the polar ice were to melt, the sea would rise many metres world-wide. Many cities, like Venice shown in this picture, have been built on low lying land and so there would be the chance of permanent *flooding*.

The change in the greenhouse weather can be stopped. But only if we all change the way we live. It is very difficult to choose between power today or disaster tomorrow. What do you think *you* could do to help?

New words

atmosphere
the layer of air that surrounds the Earth. Clouds only form in the lowest part of the atmosphere

barometer
an instrument for measuring the pressure of the air in the atmosphere. High pressure spells fine weather, low pressure forecasts rain, very low pressure tells of an approaching storm

blizzard
a snowstorm with very strong winds. In a blizzard it is almost impossible to see ahead because of the driving snow

breeze
a gentle movement of air too light to rustle the pages of an open book

cirrus
a wispy form of cloud that forms in a clear sky. Cirrus cloud is very high in the sky and made entirely of ice crystals

cloud
water droplets or ice crystals that form in the air above the ground

condensation
the formation of water droplets on a cold surface

cumulonimbus
tall rain-bearing thunderclouds

cumulus clouds
pillow-like clouds that can give showery weather

cyclone
a name given to a tropical storm with severe winds

dew
condensation that forms on leaves and other surfaces overnight

drizzle
a form of light rain with small drops

drought
a period which is dry for longer than usual and when people, plants or animals start to suffer

evaporation
the way water changes from droplets to vapour

equator
the line that divides the Earth equally in two and is half way between the poles.

fog
cloud at ground level. In a fog there are so many water droplets that it is impossible to see more than a few tens of metres

fossil fuel
the fuels such as oil, coal and gas that are obtained from under the surface of the Earth

frost
air or ground temperature that falls below 0 °C

gale
wind that is severe enough to capsize small boats

hail
a mixture of ice and water in the form of a ball-shaped lump. Hailstones only fall from thunderstorms

hurricane
a word for a tropical storm

lightning
the spark that occurs when electricity passes from a cloud to the ground or between layers in a cloud. Fork lightning occurs when you see the spark; sheet lightning is the reflection of the spark

mist
a thin form of fog. Usually you can see for more than a hundred metres but you cannot see any distant object

moisture
the word for water vapour in the air

pole
the north and south poles lie farthest away from the equator. They are places of extreme cold

precipitation
any form of water or ice that falls from a cloud. It includes rain, hail, drizzle, snow and sleet

sleet
a partly melted form of snow

stratus cloud
thick, heavy flat clouds, often with ragged rolls of cloud below. They belong to areas of low pressure and storms

snow, snowflake
ice crystals that have formed into large groups to make a snowflake, and many snowflakes fall as snow

storm force wind
a wind that is so strong it can damage buildings as well as capsize ships at sea

thermometer
the instrument used to measure temperature. It is marked in degrees Celsius, shown as °C, for short

thunder
the sound that is heard when a flash of lightning occurs. The thunder is made by the air as it is quickly heated by the lightning spark

tropics
the lands that lie either side of the equator and where the Sun shines directly overhead at least once a year

typhoon
a term for a tropical storm

water vapour
the word for the moisture in the air

weather
the day to day nature of the air. Weather is measured by temperature, windiness, cloud, sunshine and moisture

wind
the flow of air over the Earth's surface. Usually it is measured in metres per second

Index